THE KEY FORMULAS OF SUCCESSFUL ENTREPRENEURSHIP

ESSENTIAL LAWS EVERY BUSINESS OWNER MUST MASTER

JUDE ONYEKA OBUSEH

DEDICATION

This book is dedicated to both aspiring and
established entrepreneurs

CONTENTS

Preamble

Law 1 - Spot A Lacuna And Fill It

Law 2 – Develop A Stratagem

Law 3 – Master Your Craft

Law 4 – Reach Out For Help

Law 5 – Stand Out, Be Seen

Law 6 – Motivate Your Foot Soldiers

Law 7 – Build Bridges - Network

Law 8 - Treat Your Patrons As Royalty

Law 9 – Be Frugal With Your Resources

Law 10 – Do Not Overstretch Yourself

Law 11 – You Are Fighting A War – Be Battle-Ready

Law 12 – Live Your Venture - Let It drive You

Preamble

The impact of the financial catastrophes that have serially ravaged the world's economies since the dawn of the 21st century – brought about by rising interest rates, stock market crashes, and asset bubbles – include sharp decline in economic activities, decreased productivity, global inequality and poverty, depreciation in income, lower output by companies, falling purchasing power as well as consumption capacity, job loses, etc.

Consequent to the negative multiplier effects on the global economic ecosystem occasioned by these crises, consumers have drastically reduced their spending, which has culminated in decreasing demand for the products and services sold by producers, leading to job losses. This has resulted in a boom in the number of individuals planning to start their businesses as a means of escaping the emerging harsh economic realities. Compared to a few years ago, the number of individuals veering into private business has increased exponentially due largely to the sense of competition engendered by these sad developments.

Most people veer into business expecting to immediately start raking in wads of cash, only to discover that making money from a business is much more difficult than they initially thought. They come to the shocking realization that succeeding in business is not a tea party. This heartache can be avoided in business if business owners take their time in planning out all the necessary steps they need to achieve success in their enterprise.

Businesses – big or small – are susceptible to challenges that could militate against their success and growth. Some of these challenges include unfavourable government policies, high taxes, high cost of production, infrastructural challenges, lack of technical knowhow or support, poor access to raw materials, lack of capital, etc.

However, while the aforementioned challenges could be construed as significant stumbling blocks to the growth and ultimate success of a business, the principal underlying reason why businesses fail is often overlooked: Businesses fail largely because their owners disobey certain fundamental laws or principles. These entrepreneurs travel through the mazy trajectories of the business world without road maps and compasses to guard them, blindly walking into fusty cul-de-sacs.

Just as no institution can be set up and successfully administered without some Codes of Conduct guiding the conduct of its affairs, no business venture can succeed without adherence to some fundamental laws or rules. Businesses of all sizes – whether large, small, or medium scale – are guided by the same set of principles.

"The Key Formulas Of Successful Entrepreneurship: Essential Laws Every Business Owner Must Master", simplistically highlights and explains the fundamental rules of business, most of which are not amenable to casual observation. These rules are universal, in nature, and have been tested and tried from antiquity till date and have not been found wanting. But regrettably, few entrepreneurs discover and master these fundamental laws, which account for the disparity between successful businesses and failed ones. This book exposes these key principles by proffering answers to the following questions: What are the fundamental laws for building a successful business brand? Why are these laws hidden from casual observation? Why do some businesses succeed while others fail? How can these laws be applied? What are the reversals to these laws?

This book is a sort of handbook on the secret principles of successful entrepreneurship. The laws contained in this book are based on one simple principle: your chances of succeeding in any venture are increased by certain actions, while others decrease it and might even ruin the business in the long run. These laws are omnipotent and infinite.

This book can be utilized in two ways: you can either read it to learn about how to succeed in business or peruse it to examine the particular principle that best serves a particular purpose of immediate significance. Read and be illuminated!

LAW 1

SPOT A LACUNA AND FILL IT

VERDICT: *Even nature avoids a vacuum*

Starting a business usually goes through some crucial stages, ranging from conception to execution: What ideas are practicable? How can these ideas be executed? What resources are required? When is the right time to start? Becoming a successful entrepreneur requires a lot of originality and creativity. The difference between an ordinary idea and a brilliant one is the possibility of transforming it into a profitable enterprise.

God imbued us with the ability to make observations, store information, scrutinize facts, and transform them into tangible outcomes. Humans can look back to the past, interrogate the present, envision the future, strategize, and ultimately take action. The point is that everybody has ideas bubbling inside them. But sadly, most ideas remain inert until discovered and channeled towards productive ends.

Some people have erroneously fingered the lack of viable business ideas as a major challenge to becoming entrepreneurs. Funny enough, these people live in areas full of vast money-making opportunities waiting to be exploited. However, due to ignorance about the existence of these opportunities, alongside the lack of resources and the requisite know-how to implement these ideas, they have remained largely untapped. Vast money-making opportunities are staring at us everywhere we look. Aspiring entrepreneurs can tap into these vast opportunities and make the best out of them.

Under Amour in America (UARM) and the Mckesson Corporation, are two classic cases of the successful observance of **Law 1**. UARM's C.E.O, Kevin Plank, during his days as a college football player, was faced with the challenge of having to regularly swap the sweat-soaked T-shirt he wore under his jersey with a dry one. This inconvenience convinced him of the need to develop a fabric that could soak up sweat, an invention he subsequently patented as sportswear. The outfit was an instant hit in the sports community. Plank's ability to identify a specific need and transform that idea into a practical reality has transformed (UARM) into a multi-million dollar organization – a trailblazer in the global sportswear manufacturing industry.

Another inspiring example of the application of this law was that of the McKesson Corporation, an organization that was set up in 1883 to import and distribute scarce pharmaceutical products and chemicals across the United States of America. This stemmed from the conviction of the corporation's founders that it was possible to import and distribute these drugs on a wholesale scale across the country. Today, McKesson Corporation, an organization that was born in rustic Manhattan, has through the creative genius of its founders, sound strategizing, and consistency, transformed into the world's largest distributor of wholesale goods, and the fifteenth largest company in the world, generating billions of dollars annually.

The secret behind the overwhelming success of the McKesson Corporation was the solid foundation on which it was built: discovering a need and servicing that need. It set the stage for the prosperity, fame, and reverence it currently enjoys. Just like McKesson and UARM, profitable businesses – big or small – are built on solid ideas. Ideas can be generated by observing developments around you and building your business around those developments. Certain needs in the society are not being met - meet these needs. This law will bode well for both existing businesses seeking opportunities to expand, as well as startups.

However, there are several tragic cases of businesses that failed because they were constructed on impracticable ideas. Out of respect for the owners of some of these failed business concerns across the world, this writer would prefer not to name names, but advise that any budding entrepreneur should avoid rushing blindly into business without duly testing the waters. Market demands must be verified, while other factors such as capital, labour, raw materials, production capacity, and other requirements should be considered to avoid heartbreaks. Why do you want to go into your line of business? What are the demands for your products and services? Is the market for your products and service accessible? Have you done proper feasibility studies? What is your comparative advantage over your rivals in the same line of business?

This Law is very crucial for the take-off and ultimate success of any business venture.

REVERSAL: *This law has no reversal at all. It is the foundation stone of any business venture. But be warned, not all ideas are opportunities!*

LAW 2

DEVELOP A STRATAGEM

VERDICT: *People easily forget the past; you must think and envision the future*

Starting a business without adequate planning is a sure path to disaster. You must plan every step, action, and decision you make. Without adequate planning, you will not be prepared for the unexpected vagaries of business - the likely drawbacks, pitfalls, and disappointments that might scupper your efforts.

The truth is that success in business is not solely dependent on your skills and experience, but on your strategies and *modus operandi*. The reason why so many businesses fail is attributable to the absence of practicable Business Plans. In the same manner that a ship captain cannot navigate through a rough tempest to safety, without a properly functioning compass and rudder, no business can succeed without a well-crafted plan. This is where a solid business plan becomes expedient.

A well-scripted business plan is like a compass that helps you navigate through the murky waters of the business world to the shores of success. It keeps you on course and prevents you from sailing off into violent waters. Like an early-warning system, it alerts you of impending danger by sounding the alarm bells when it seems you are losing focus and deviating from your core objectives. It is the manifesto containing the statement of intent and line of action of your business.

A business plan helps you construct and streamline a strategy for starting or varying your business; it defines how you will achieve your most significant business objectives; it defines the viability of a business idea before putting much effort and resources into it; it warns you of possible pitfalls and how to avoid them, and the resources required to achieve your business goals as well as when and how these resources can/should be deployed.

A tactical business model usually contains the mission, vision, and objectives (long and short-term) of your business: Where would you like your company to be in one, five, or ten years? What would you like the income statement of your company to read at the end of one, five, or ten years? How large would you like your company to ultimately become? How much are you willing to invest in your business at its inception and in subsequent years? What are your Competitive Strategies? What are your Profit and Cost analyses for each business segment? What is your Marketing Plan? What is your Human Resources Plan? What is your facilities' Plan? What is your Customer Service Plan? What is your Financial Plan?

The merits of having a business plan are legion as it can illuminate the decision-making process concerning salient aspects of the business such as capital investments, human capital, resourcing, etc. A well-crafted business model helps you define your key business objectives to work towards. Are you seeking credit from a bank or money from financiers, you require a business model that answers multiple questions.

Staff recruitment is another area where having a solid business plan could come in handy. Without any doubt, no business can succeed and grow without a talented pool of workers animating its affairs. Recruiting the right talent, at crucial moments, is a vital aspect of a business plan's objective. Employees with the right vision and mindset of the trajectories a business intends to travel will contribute their best towards helping realize this objective.

Again, for a business to have structure and defined administrative objectives, it must have a plan, which will become a reference instrument to keeping the business on track with its primary objectives. It is simply a list of your company's projected projects and their expected outcomes. When you properly plan and execute your business plans, success is guaranteed.

A business with a well-crafted plan enables the business owner to see into the future "with as much clarity as the legendary "gods on Mount Olympus" – it enables you to see several steps ahead and plan your strategies sequentially. Like a Chess grandmaster, you will not be in a quandary when serious challenges rear their ugly heads as your clearly defined plans will shield you from the hiccups and heartaches that are the major reasons why many promising ventures falter and ultimately collapse.

If you own an existing business, regularly update your business plans – possibly on an annual basis – to keep track of its growth and determine whether there are fresh opportunities to exploit.

REVERSAL: *This law is omnipotent. It is the brain of any business. Other laws rest on it, for without a comprehensive plan your business is as good as dead. Adequate planning is the key to success in any venture. No serious general can lead his army into battle without a proper battle plan – it would be suicidal.*

LAW 3

MASTER YOUR CRAFT

VERDICT: *It takes patience, discipline, and consistency to become successful at something; learn to master your craft*

You cannot excel in what you do not know. The surest way to know is to learn from those who already know. In the social sciences, a newborn baby is referred to as a Tabula Rasa - a blank slate; an empty shell. But through the process of socialization, this clean slate learns the norms, values, and expected roles as a potential member of society. The process of socialization is a kind of weaning period for every member of any human society; it is a period of social apprenticeship during which social skills are learned and internalized.

Success in any enterprise, business or otherwise, depends on how much you know about the business you are involved in or interested in. You can't become a successful manufacturer if you don't understand the fundamentals of the manufacturing business: Location, skills, market, etc. Can a Bank Manager become a successful automobile dealer overnight without learning the trade? Of course not! You cannot excuse your failure on the grounds of ignorance.

The knowledge you have about your business is one of your greatest assets – it compliments other factors of production. You have a choice to decide whether your business fails or succeeds by placing first things first. Nobody knows it all. Those who seem to know so much were thought by those who also learned from others. The learning process is an infinite chain – a continuum. Do not develop a penchant for always wanting to do it alone – it is dangerous. Reaching out to others is the safest, most proper, most potent tactical move.

Therefore, for your business to succeed and remain successful, it is wise that you consult those who have been in your line of business for tips. Most businesses fail because their owners lack the basic knowledge of what they are supposed to do. This most times stems from excessive pride or fear that someone else will steal their idea, or simply do not know that help is accessible. Availing yourself of available help will open you up to more opportunities, help you keep an eye out for new networking opportunities no matter where you are, and make you wiser in taking decisions like recruitment and long-term collaborations.

There are small business owners who are willing to share their success secrets with you as far as you are not an immediate competitor or rival. But if you do not find people ready to help you with tips, you can take up employment in an organization that offers similar services in your area of business interest, earn some money and gain some priceless practical experience. The point is that just like a military General embarking on a military campaign, a business General must be versed in his trade if he wishes to overcome the several landmines that the world of the entrepreneur is strewn with, for the world of business is not different from a state of war. Just like in war, business involves a lot of tactical maneuverings. The more knowledge you have about your business, the better you are at taking crucial decisions that will ultimately determine either its success or failure.

Again, an aspiring entrepreneur can carry out private, in-depth research into what some other people in their line of business have done in the past by reading books, watching movies and documentaries, attending business seminars and workshops, and listening to tapes and other recordings or works on the lives and business strategies of successful entrepreneurs. How and why did these people succeed in their businesses? What were/are their business secrets? You can borrow their success secrets to make headway in your line of business. You can also do the same for people who failed in the same line of business: What was the cause of their failure? Did they make mistakes, or where they victims of circumstances beyond their control? By learning from their mistakes you will be able to avoid any pitfall that rears itself in your line of business.

True creativity does not occur in a vacuum. Great minds like Bill Gates, Warren Buffet, Jeff Bezos, Aliko Dangote, William Shakespeare, Steve Jobs, Chinua Achebe, Wole Soyinka, Amilca Cabral, Galileo Galilei, Mazisi Kunene, etc, were inspired by the great souls who passed the baton to them – their mentors or giants. If you want to succeed in life, you must admit the fact that you do not know everything and that you have to learn from others to reach your goals. Every successful man was inspired by someone else.

Any aspiring entrepreneur must endeavor to learn from the pioneers, trailblazers, role models, partners, vendors, and peers in their line of enterprise – their inputs will help you achieve your long-term vision. Like a preying vulture, you can profit from their hard work.

REVERSAL: *Always be on top of your business. Do not swallow hook, line, and sinker everything you see others do or hear them say. Despite the utilitarian value of good advice, your ideas should be omnipotent.*

LAW 4

REACH OUT FOR HELP

VERDICT: *Dispersal is a crucial strategy in guerilla warfare; business warfare is no exception.*

You may have passion for the business that you are planning to start, but can you afford the business? Is the cost of the business within your grasp? Where will you secure funds to support your production, marketing, and operations?

From close observation it is quite obvious why some new businesses fail at their embryonic stages – they Lack "CAPITAL". Without money, your business has no life. Any business without capital is doomed to fail. Capital is the lifeblood that fuels revenue-generating businesses. Raising capital is the greatest huddle entrepreneurs' face in their quest for success.

Some of the stumbling blocks that militate against adequate capital mobilization include pride, ignorance, and reluctance on the part of the business owner to source funds outside what he has. Some budding entrepreneurs are most times ruled by their egos. They do not want to be seen as beggarly, so they refrain from asking for help from certain persons, be they friends, family members, or other acquaintances. However, some individuals are not simply aware that help is available everywhere. Their idea of business is confined to the popular dogma of buying, selling, and profit-making. Nothing else matters to this set of entrepreneurs.

At the take-off stage of your business, when capital is limited or simply not available, it is advisable to reach out to all available sources of funding. What do you gain by isolating yourself from available help? Practically nothing! There are people out there looking for viable projects to invest in or support. Sort them out and utilize their funds for your business. Funds can be sourced via Self-Funding/Bootstrapping, Partnership, Crowd Funding, Angel Investment, Venture Capital, Bank Loans, and other accessible sources.

Self-Funding is the most common source of funding for most businesses and should be the first option for startups. It is easier to raise funds through this avenue as there are fewer formalities/compliance plus lesser costs and flexible interest rates attached to such loans. Personal savings and loans from family and friends can come in handy here. To convince them to support you show them your plan for the business as well as your passion and you are assured of their support. It is as simple as that.

You can also approach **Angel Investors** for funds. Angels Investors are rich individuals with wads of cash to spare who are interested in supporting startups with potential. You can put up a solid business proposal that can convince them to invest in your business. Some global giants were funded by Angel Investors at their takeoff points.

Again, you can also enter into **Partnerships** with like-minded people. You could approach some of your affluent friends and present your business initiative to them and convince them to come into a partnership with you by investing some of their spare funds in the venture. You let them know that they would be co-owners of the business. You work out a profit-sharing arrangement with them in which you will be the one running the business on their behalf. You run the business, earn your percentage as the brain of the business and pay them their commissions as and when due.

Another fundraising strategy is **Crowd-Funding** which has been gaining popularity in recent times. It involves setting up an investment platform with a large pool of contributors. Your crowd-funding platform will contain a description of your business, listing the objectives, profit projections, projected budget, purpose, etc. Interested clients could be interested in your business plan and make their contributions in the form of pledges or outright donations. People are disposed to assisting businesses they believe have potential. One of the major advantages of Crowd-Funding is that it provides funds for startups by bypassing formal investment channels.

Venture Capital and **Bank Loans** are some of the other fundraising strategies budding entrepreneurs can access to execute their business plans. A venture capital investment is better suited for businesses that are already generating impressive income. Bank Loans, which were the most common source of capital for business, remain significant sources of funds for entrepreneurs. To access a bank loan it is advised that you work out the size of the loan you need commensurate with your business plan (See Law 2), research the banks, and approach the one you choose with your business plan and other personal financial requirements.

By leveraging on any or a combination of these aforementioned fundraising strategies, capital can be mobilized for the smooth and solid take-off of your business. Capital is the base of any business venture, large or small-scale. It is the elixir that keeps businesses going. Without it, no business can survive.

REVERSAL: *Reasonable as it sounds, you must very be careful of the nature of loans you obtain for your business. Bad loans kill businesses in the long run due to the conditions attached to them. Endeavour to confirm the conditions attached to any loan you seek to avoid future regrets. In the case of partnerships, avoid greedy and impatient investors – they can stymie your* *business and ultimately tear it apart.*

LAW 5

STAND OUT, BE SEEN

VERDICT: *Be a spectacle, your appearance matters; endeavor to stand out*

One of the reasons why businesses fail is because they do not have faces of their own - nothing distinguishes them from other businesses. A business without a face of its own is seriously limited in its drive for success. A business can grow faster if it has distinguishing features. This is where branding plays a very critical role in the growth of a business.

What is a brand? A brand is simply the promise a business makes to its clients – It tells them what they should expect to benefit from patronizing its products or services. A brand stand's out from the crowd; It is exquisite, profound, and unique.

Brands can also be established through the creation and operation of a fluid, proactive, aggressive, target-driven, and sustained service delivery mechanism. That giant multinationals spend billions annually to reinforce their brands underscores the importance of branding to the success of a business.

Just like large corporations, small businesses can also build and strengthen their brands. You can transform your products and services into genuine brands using the following strategies: Identifying your unique selling points (USP); creating a connection between your product and the customers who use it; creating a name, logo, and slogan for your brand; staying consistent with your brand; and enjoying the cheap and easy approach.

Your USP sets your brand apart from others in the same line of business. What distinguishes Nike from Adidas, Under Amour, Admiral, and other sportswear manufacturers? Why do people in Africa prefer DSTV to others, or Coke to other cola products? Make serious efforts to identify and strengthen your USP. Also, ensure you practice what you preach and deliver on whatever you promise your customers.

Again, your products and services must be targeted at a particular market – they must connect with a particular audience. This can be done through the Identification of a select group of people and targeting them as your customers – students, youths, celebrities, elderly, women, men, sports personalities, etc. If you do not properly target your products and services at a particular market, you are not likely to command large patronage and subsequent loyalty from your customers (**See Laws 1 and 2**). To achieve this, you must carry out detailed research. Find out the prospects of this niche in the market and identify its weaknesses: What is your target market like? What can you do to serve them as a group and as individuals? But do not expect instant results – you must be patient. First, offer your consumers your products and services, make them your loyal patrons, and ultimately they will stick to your brand like glue.

On the other hand, you must create a name, logo, and slogan for your brand, which must be catchy and evergreen to create the desired effect(s). Your business name should invoke your brand's aura whenever it is mentioned, just as your slogan, which is the face of your business, should have pictographic effects on prospective clients. Brands like Honda, Mercedes, Addidas, Coca-Cola, MTN, Amazon, etc, have magical effects on the public.

However, care must be taken not to constantly modify the distinguishing features of your brand; there is need to maintain some consistency. You cannot afford to have different names, logos, and slogans within a few years. It just doesn't make sense. That is not to say you cannot make strategic alterations in the quality of your products and services, marketing strategy, management drive, advertisement stratagem, etc. You can make these improvements without altering the distinguishing features of your business.

In all, your business needs a face of its own to gain, increase, keep its customers, stay afloat, and maintain profitability.

REVERSAL: *No reversal to this law. Your business must have a distinguishing face of its own to succeed.*

LAW 6

MOTIVATE YOUR FOOT SOLDIERS

VERDICT: *Every labourer desires to be appreciated*

This author disagrees completely with the so-called conventional wisdom that financial motivation (alone) encourages industry. It is not always the case as some practical, everyday examples have shown. No amount of monetary compensation can replace sincere words of appreciation. We are ready to go the extra mile for anybody or organization that shows appreciation for our efforts.

The productivity of your staff is determined to a large extent by how positively psyched up they are to work for you. Money of course is important, but it should not take the place of gratitude. Otherwise, your staff will begin to see themselves as mere human robots being exploited for profit, and become withdrawn from their work, ultimately resulting in poor output.

You must strive to instill a sense of worth in your staff. They must be made to enjoy the work they do for you; must feel a sense of accomplishment after performing their tasks. The jobs they do for you must become part of them; something they look up to doing every day; something they live, talk, eat, drink, sleep, and dream. Encourage them, and they will in turn work for the success of your business.

Another added incentive is to promote exceptional performers. You can locate these excellent performers by testing them. Once you find them, assign them very challenging duties you know they can carry out smoothly, praise them for their efforts when they do, and assign them new ones. Do not let your criticism be over-flogged, even when they err. Let them know exactly why you are criticizing them, what you expect of them, and endeavor to follow up each rebuke with words of appreciation for previous good deeds. When you accommodate your staff they will sweat for your success.

Motivating your employees is a very effective psychological strategy for obtaining the best from them, as it will ultimately culminate in the phenomenal growth of your business. Just like the psychological tool of 'Classical Conditioning', which emphasizes constantly influencing humans or animals to perform identical actions until they becomes used to them, a consistently well-motivated staff becomes naturally more effective at what they do. They begin to see themselves in what they do and strive to put in their best to satisfy not only their bosses but themselves.

Great football coaches, for instance, are masters of the art of motivation. They have uncanny abilities for bringing out the best in their players. Apart from their technical and tactical inputs, coupled with the hefty pay packets their players command, the psychological techniques employed by these tacticians, in the management of their players, are their key strengths. These geniuses inculcate self-belief into their players; convictions in the possibility of being the best that they can be. This belief system ultimately transforms into a winning philosophy; a philosophy that produces a mindset that nothing is impossible for the bold and committed, those who dare to defy the odds, no matter how formidable. Ambitious entrepreneurs can borrow a leaf from the motivational and man-managerial skills of football grandmasters such as Jose Mourhino, Sir Alex Ferguson, Pep Guardiola, Arsene Wenger, etc.

The point being made here is that monetary rewards alone aren't just enough motivation for your staff. You must constantly think up new and more appealing ways to inspire and challenge your staff. You can set high goals for them, stir up competition, keep records, and then reward the exceptional ones in cash and kind. Encourage them to see themselves as co-owners of the business, and they will get you the stars.

In all, monetary compensation cannot buy complete loyalty. But every human being likes to be appreciated for good deeds, especially by those they work for. Thus apart from monetary incentives, which are also necessary, business owners should develop a penchant for frequently appreciating their exceptional employees. The truth is that nothing else can replace a few appropriate, timely, genuine words of gratitude – they are absolutely priceless.

REVERSAL: *However, in applying this law, do not become too predictable. The catchphrase is "appreciate the contributions of your employees to the growth of your company" in a calculated manner.*

LAW 7

BUILD BRIDGES – NETWORK

VERDICT: *Do not be an island to yourself – a tree cannot make a forest*

All the members of your workforce constitute very significant components of your organization: from the cleaner, security man, crane operator, gardener, janitor, and manager. Other critical components of this system include your partners/shareholders, customers, and other stakeholders. These are people with some very priceless information, suggestions and solutions to some often overlooked challenges in your organization. But these actors will not just come forward with valuable information if you do not solicit advice or create avenues for them to open up to you.

Some organizations, especially large-scale enterprises are too rigid, personalized, and closed in their relations with their staff. Take the case of the Chief Executive Officer (C.E.O) of a conglomerate who considers himself superior to the junior staff, and thus, does not see eye-to-eye with them. Hierarchically run companies like these are bound to lose valuable information. Some small-scale entrepreneurs are guilty of bringing their egos into the running of their businesses. They live under the false belief that relating too much with their staff will breed contempt. Due to this superiority complex, you never see them joke, chat or even solicit any kind of information from their employees. This poor attitude constitutes a major pitfall to the success of such brands.

The guys in the field interacting with customers — the foot soldiers – are very key to the success of your business. You must endeavor to romance them. Your business associates are your third eye who can see what you do not see and can alert you of dangerous pitfalls. With these extra sets of eyes, you become like "Janus", the double-faced Roman Deity, able to see from different perspectives and make better-informed decisions.

Mathew McCauley, the young CEO of

Gymboree (GYMB), in San Francisco, California, USA was able to significantly boost the company's sales by soliciting feedback from staffers, regardless of their position in the company. According to him, he loved to rub minds with the company's customers, clients and other related stakeholders. He believes every employee of the company is unique in their own way and have something to offer. This is coming from a visionary leader who, since taking over the running of the company, has boosted sales to high heavens by employing one of the most often overlooked success tricks: seeking out the truth from those who know.

Customers should also be considered in this wise. As the end consumers or users of your products and services, they are better suited to telling you what they like or do not like about your products and services. With the information elicited from them, you can strategize on ways of improving your products and services. Create an interactive, dynamic, mobile, flexible, and fluid feedback mechanism in your organization, and you will reap stupendous dividends from the large cache of information you will have at your disposal to prosecute your business wars.

Employees and customers are very crucial stakeholders in your business. They are your allies. Without their vital contributions, your business is as good as dead. They fend off the missiles fired at your business by your competitors, point out your strengths and weaknesses, and warn you of impending pitfalls. Bringing them into your confidence is like forming an unbreakable phalanx that cannot be penetrated by even the most resilient adversary; that is, your competitors who want to whittle down your turf and kick you out of business.

In a nutshell, make yourself accessible to your associates – staff, partners, customers, etc. Keep your ears to the ground, and always listen to what they tell you.

REVERSAL: *Always be on top of every situation. Don't be in a hurry to swallow every bit of suggestion or information you elicit from others. Subject them to critical analysis— separate the wheat from the chafe— before making any tactical move. Look before you leap. After all, it is your business you are running.*

LAW 8

TREAT YOUR PATRONS AS ROYALTY

VERDICT: *Customers are always right, without them you have no business*

Your "Customer is King". This hoary refrain expresses the indispensability of customers/consumers to the success of any business – large or small. The truth is that every business is targeted at a market – your customer base without which your business cannot exist in the first place. Meeting and exceeding the expectations of your customers is very crucial to the success and continued growth of your business. By constantly putting your customers before any other consideration, your business' success, growth, and survival are guaranteed.

Every entrepreneur must constantly seek out

ways to meet or exceed the expectations of their clients. If you do, they will keep coming back and asking for more like Oliver Twist. Just keep giving them what they want — even go the extra mile. Make them the centerpiece of your business. Accept your mistakes, correct them, apologize, take responsibility for your actions, and ensure that their satisfaction is always guaranteed.

Your business is not complete until your customers are satisfied with your products or services, and the only way their satisfaction can be guaranteed is by prompt delivery to meet their needs. Respecting customers' values is the only way to ensure their loyalty to your brand.

The case of Nordstrom is a classic case of how to guarantee and exceed your customers' satisfaction. Nordstrom is one of the pacesetters in the department store business in the United States of America (U.S.A). One of its success secrets is that customers' values are placed above every other consideration as extra efforts are made to treat them like royalty. While shopping at Nordstrom, customers are made comfortable by being treated to soft music, served drinks and hot meals. This, coupled with their lavish, liberal risk limitation offers, has given them a strategic advantage over their rivals, gobbling up large chunks of the retail market in the process.

Compare this with the case of some other retail shops where the values of customers are ignored. The first impression one gets on entering these stores is the pompous and withdrawn mien of their proprietors. They ignore you when you greet them and harshly demand to know what you are looking for. The sales attendants are not better off. They busy themselves with personal concerns, not caring to attend to their customers' needs. Theirs is a classic case of customer (dis) service of the most atavistic kind. No sane person will return to such a shop next time even if they are giving out free meals. This problem is common with most struggling businesses and accounts for the poor patronage of their products and services, and in extreme cases, their ultimate total collapse.

Laziness, poor communication, bad attitude, lack of commitment, lack of knowledge, attending to customers on "auto-pilot" and lack of professionalism, are all barriers to excellent customer service and should be jettisoned by any serious-minded entrepreneur. Strengthening the customer care aspects of your business will go a long way in increasing its profit margins and ensuring continued patronage from customers.

The fundamentals of effective customer service are confidentiality, attention, integrity, reliability, respect/courtesy, prompt service, accuracy, support, empathy, understanding, flexibility, service recovery, etc. Adherence to these crucial principles will impact positively on businesses through increased customer loyalty, word-of-mouth advertising, increase in revenue and profit, better financial performance, and competitive edge.

Treat your customers like very important personalities (VIPs), and they will reciprocate by pledging their undying loyalty to your brand. Customers can be easily manipulated – play along with them, discover their thumbscrews, and twist them to your advantage. Always act like you are concerned for their welfare. Make it a point to always listen to their complaints, and make a show of attending to them, and the invisible paymaster will continue to bombard your accounts with loads of cash.

REVERSAL: *Do not over-apply this law. Customers become wary when they feel you are trying too hard to please them. They may begin to see your gestures of honesty and generosity as smokescreens for ulterior motives; your gifts might then be seen as Trojan Horses, with hidden obligations. Be natural with your customers. Make your gestures simple, and effortless. But the fact remains that your customers are omnipotent. Without them, you don't have a business. Rub their backs and they will rub yours in return.*

LAW 9

BE FRUGAL WITH YOUR RESOURCES

VERDICT: *A rich man is he who earns more than he spends, and not a man whose expense is not commensurate with his desires*

Any entrepreneur who wishes to maintain a competitive edge over his competitors must be schooled in the art of managing expenses. Most businessmen in the modern era focus too much on the moneymaking end of their businesses without a corresponding focus on their most priceless asset: the efficient management of the cost of running that business. This is one of the major reasons why so many promising start-ups fold up after just a few stuttering attempts.

A business owner can make mistakes and not be adversely affected if properly schooled in the art of expense management. It has nothing to do with smartness, but how financially suave you are. Financial savvy is one of the keys to the success of any business venture. The challenge of expense management is a challenge worth mastering. There are no blanket approaches to expense management, but there are some guidelines that can be applied to any organization which would be helpful in achieving set goals. The following expense management tips will aid the entrepreneur in his quest to turn his business into a profitable one.

First and foremost, a fluid line of communication between the management and staff of a company must be established and maintained at all times for proper expense management. The truth is that the only way company staff can conform to expense policies is if they know what these policies are and the purpose they are meant to serve. It is pertinent that any employee with access to the company's exchequer is versed in what is allowed and what is not. This should be the standard practice. Communicating your organization's policies to your staff, without assumptions, will make them know what is expected of them. This is a crucial strategy that should be imbibed by any serious business owner.

Again, you must gain financial literacy. This is one of the key foundations of any successful business venture. Most entrepreneurs are in too much of a hurry to make money and forget to lay this most crucial of foundations. Thus, they fail to equip themselves with the most critical tool for the success of their business. They forget that business is not all about how much turnover your operation makes, but what you can count as profit after all expenses, from sales, production and running costs, and other expenditure are factored in; that is, what your income statement reads in juxtaposition with your balance sheet. Have you expended more on the business than you have made from it? Do you know what your income statement truly reads? Knowing how to study and comprehend figures is vital to the success of your business.

Related to financial literacy is the need to imbibe a savings culture. Do not consume all the income your business makes. This is the only way you can make progress in your business. A businessman who spends all his profits without saving some of it is on a sure trip to failure. Spending all you make puts pressure on your business as you will then have to work very hard to maintain solvency. It is advisable to reserve a particular percentage of your profits for the security and continued existence of your business, keeping in mind the fact you are in business for profit. If, for example, your business rakes in five hundred thousand dollars ($500,000) monthly, you can make provision to save, let us say, about forty (60%) of that amount. Any genuine entrepreneur must possess a large dose of financial habitude.

You must also make proper use of your Departmental Heads – the Generals of your army – by delegating some powers to them. Through regular meetings, you can impress upon them how crucial they are to the management of the company's expense regime. Encourage them with incentives and other freebies and they will help you plug leakages you did not know existed. Learn to effectively utilize your departmental heads – they are your principal expense assets.

Again, you must imbibe a habit of speedy compensation for your workforce, even when you are cash-strapped. A situation whereby employees are owed salaries and other entitlements for months, even years, tends to create bad blood between them and management. Employees expect to be paid promptly for services rendered. It is their entitlement. That is why business owners must develop a fluid process that ensures that all requests are expeditiously attended to.

Regularly Auditing your company's expense account is another point worth highlighting. The merits of auditing a company's expense account are legion, some of which are that it will save you money, keep track of all employee expenses, and ensure that your financial records are always in order; it is a compulsory practice that helps prevent worst-case scenarios. However, audits should only be done as and when necessary, in tandem with the requirements of your business, and in such a manner that it does not negatively impinge on the service delivery capability of your workforce.

Other strategies for keeping tabs on your expenses include smart use of reports, creating and activating a reasonable appeal system, staying in tune with industry standards, etc.

REVERSAL: *There is no reversal to this law. You must manage your finances for your business to grow. Anything contrary to this is a sure part to business collapse.*

LAW 10

DO NOT OVERSTRETCH YOURSELF

VERDICT: *Focus on your point of comparative advantage, do not dissipate your energy and resources on unprofitable ventures.*

What quality does the successful have that the unsuccessful lacks? Why do some succeed while others fail? The difference between these sets of individuals is their level of focus. Thus, the businessman, who learns to focus on his business, will ultimately master and succeed in it. Focusing and mastering your business is one of the surest routes to successful entrepreneurship.

The truth is that once your business starts growing there is always the temptation to veer into other Profit-making ventures, a move that might harm your core business as you are likely to lose focus and no longer be able to deliver satisfactory customer service. For instance, in 1967, Foremost acquired the McKesson Corporation and attempted to fashion out a company consisting of two alien businesses without a clear-cut policy plank. This resulted in a sharp fall in the company's revenue – a logical consequence of the faceless and directionless posture of the new venture.

This is characteristic of some businesses, especially small ones. This largely stems from too much greed on the part of the owners of these businesses for profit. As soon as they start making some profit from their business, they venture into other seemingly profitable ones. Thus, you find a single person manufacturing bottled water, selling building materials, importing electronic gadgets, selling essential commodities, and manufacturing paint. How can these jumbled-up, unrelated businesses succeed?

A serious-minded businessman must not wander from business to business, or be distracted from the stated mission, vision, and objectives of his enterprise. He must learn to concentrate and stay connected to growing his business. Losing focus and dissipating his energies in other ventures outside his own is a sure route to collapse. Successful entrepreneurship is measured in terms of intensity, not extensity; quality, not quantity. When you allow yourself to be distracted by other concerns outside your primary area of focus, you lose concentration, which might be detrimental to the overall success and growth of your business. Concentrate on your business, and wrestle it to submission.

The practical truth is that you cannot hit two targets with just one arrow. Once you stray from the stated objectives of your business, your business is in deep waters. You must stay focused. It is quite unfortunate that many entrepreneurs attempt to have their fingers in all pies and inevitably get burnt in the process. Focusing on your business gives it direction - a smooth path to success.

You may also have to assess the unprofitable aspects of your business. Is the cost of production commensurate with your profit? Are you spending too much on advertising, transportation, remuneration and marketing? If there are aspects of your business that are draining your resources, it is advisable to review them and concentrate your resources on more profitable ones. This route was followed in 1976 by the McKesson Corporation. Consequent to a change of guards that brought in Neil Harlan as President, in 1983, some surgery was carried out on the organization to shore up its profitability. This took the form of selling off 11 of its underperforming subsidiaries to raise capital. By focusing on its core business— healthcare wholesale distribution— the company is now more able to meet the healthcare needs of its customers, consequently becoming the 15th largest company in the world.

Just like the McKesson Group and other thriving global brands, small and medium-scale enterprises can become successful by concentrating on their strongest points – their areas of comparative advantage. They should avoid the temptation of branching off into other businesses for the mere sake of it.

REVERSAL: *Although it is advisable to focus on only profitable businesses, there are times when dispersion is necessary, especially when opportunities to reduce your cost of production rear their heads. For instance, a poultry farmer can* *significantly reduce his cost of production and generate extra income by going into the production of poultry feeds and other related agro-allied products. Wise as dispersion is, it should not be carried out to extreme lengths but should be done only when necessary, and after careful stocktaking.*

LAW 11

YOU ARE FIGHTING A WAR – BE BATTLE-READY

VERDICT: *To win a war, you must first identify your adversary*

The wealth creation process is highly competitive – it is warfare. Business wars could be normal competitions or, in extreme cases, unprovoked attempts by bigger businesses to gobble up or control smaller ones.

Humans compete daily. From those setting up new ventures or strengthening already existing ones, entrepreneurs must be alert to the devices of their rivals, to prevent heartaches. If you are not aware of your competitor's moves, you cannot devise strategies to counter them and maintain your competitive edge. That is why every business must have a comprehensive plan (**see Law 2**) which must include a section dedicated to competitive analysis.

A competitive analysis affords you the opportunity of closely observing what your rival is up to and why. It contains a list of your main competitors, their strengths, and weaknesses. The more information you have about them, the better prepared you are to do battle with them: Where are they located? What are their products/services? What do their products/services cost? What are their marketing strategies, messages, web addresses, and reputations?

The major reason why clever entrepreneurs succeed in their business, and their success seems extraordinary, is their foreknowledge of their competitors' strategies. This foreknowledge cannot be warmed out of ghosts, diviners, fortune tellers, prophets, or Brahmins. It must be obtained by careful intelligence work – through artful spying. In business parlance, it is called the art of "shopping your competition". This can be done by finding out their lines of business, making inquiries from them on the phone, visiting their locations, befriending their staff, interacting with their clients to ascertain their impressions about your rivals, buying their products or requesting their services, obtaining their price lists and counting customers entering and exiting their facilities, alongside other strategies aimed at extracting crucial intelligence that would better prepare you for your business battles.

Artful spying is not a new strategy in warfare. In business as in military warfare, arming yourself with crucial knowledge of your competitors or opponents improves your aim in the long run. Most large corporations the world over engage in this practice in prosecuting their business wars. Through the use of moles (spies), some of these organizations obtain business secrets and use them to their advantage. Although this practice might be ethically frowned upon it is standard practice in the business world of today.

The advantage of gathering intelligence on your competition is not far-fetched, for in the realm of business, the objective of the entrepreneur is the extent of control he has over key aspects of his business. But the problem is that competing businesses will not just surrender their success secrets to you.

They control the amounts of information they let out to the public, keeping the most crucial aspects of their operations under wraps. The logical consequence is that you have access to only pockets of information, which might be deceptive and not be useful to your quest for competitive advantage. You must seek ways of warming this information out of all available sources.

With the information gathered from your spy network, you can stand up to the competition, coming up with products and services that are peculiar to your brand image. Your business will be miles ahead of the competition because of the range of information at your disposal. The products and services you design and churn out will be eclectic, having their intended original quality and significant aspects of other competing products. This leverage will ultimately shore up your customer base and strengthen the brand in the process. You pre-empt your competitors into making tactical errors, as they try agonizingly to unravel the secrets behind your success.

REVERSAL: *Crucial as it is, standing up to*

your competitors should not be carried out without recourse to legal and ethical principles guarding the conduct of business in your country. It should be done intelligently and without recourse to criminality of any kind. Also know that the law of retribution operates in the business world, for as you try to outwit your competitors, expect them to also spy on you. It is tit-for-tat.

LAW 12

LIVE YOUR VENTURE – LET IT DRIVE YOU

VERDICT: *You cannot succeed in what you do without passion for it*

Success in any venture is premised on a large dose of faith or belief. Believing is being certain of possibilities, irrespective of the odds. Passion is either inborn or learned. Anybody who aspires to be a success needs it. To succeed in business, you must believe in it more than anybody else. Through sheer passion for your business, you can overcome every single one of your shortcomings.

For a business to succeed, thrive and grow, the owner must put it before every other consideration. You must sleep, work, eat, talk, and dream about your business. It should be your center of gravity – the concentric point around which every other activity revolves.

Just like an athlete who goes the extra mile in training for an event with the hope of setting or breaking records, an entrepreneur must go the whole hog if he wishes to break even in his trade. Average people cannot be the best in their fields of endeavour. You must strive to be the reference point, the standard to beat in your line of trade.

Passionate people persist in doing whatever they set out to do, and by persisting they succeed at it. Neither talent, intellect, nor education can take the place of persistence (another word) for passion. Passion is the life force of any worthy enterprise. No venture can succeed without commensurate passion.

Most people fail to achieve success in most ventures, business inclusive, because they do not persist. That is why majority of startups collapse prematurely – their owners do not have passion; they chicken out after a few stuttering attempts. The truth is that you can only become a success at what you do when you make up your mind to, and you exclusively occupy yourself with overcoming all obstacles standing in your way to glory.

The adversary of compulsive passion is extreme fear. Fear incapacitates commitment, strangles creativity, blurs focus, and murders dreams. Several forms of fear constantly cascade through our minds, ranging from fear of heights, fear of enclosed spaces, fear of the dark, fear of infection, fear of death, fear of rodents, fear of speed, etc. These rational fears help us set boundaries on our human extremes and in making rational decisions. They are real, not concocted or imagined. But our fears, rather than preventing us from achieving our goals should be catalysts for positive growth. They are tests of our abilities, our staying power in the face of daunting challenges, and should not be viewed from fatalistic standpoints – they are not debilitating obstacles crafted from hell.

Fear of failure is the most emasculating of all fears pervading the world of the entrepreneur. Budding entrepreneurs have a choice to choose between fear and faith; between failure and success. The truth is that, whether in business or other fields of human endeavour, unfounded fear breeds failure, while unrestricted passion logically results in success. Passion (a pseudonym for faith) defeats fear, ignores danger, focuses on goals, leaps over pitfalls, and defeats obstacles. It is the undisputed cornerstone of all successes recorded by the human species from antiquity to date.

It is on record that the greatest achievers in recorded history had to overcome huge obstacles camouflaged as fear before reaching their milestones. The likes of Arch Bishop Benson Idahosa, Christopher Columbus, Muhammad Ali, Abraham Lincoln, Mahatma Gandhi, Graham Bell, Bill Gates, Nelson Mandela, David Oyedepo, Thomas Edison, Martin Luther King, etc, all had to surmount legions of obstacles cloaked as fear. These giants were faced with several discouraging challenges at different stages of their struggles. Their successes were not achieved on a bed of roses but through passionate commitment to reaching their set goals.

The difference between a successful business and a failed one is the decisions their owners make between choosing fear over faith or vice versa. A cowardly businessman avoids taking risks; he always plays it safe. Consequently, his success is confined within the limits of his fears. A passionate entrepreneur, on the other hand, is bold, resilient, focused, and result-oriented. He dares the odds, strives against the discouraging elements of his trade, and comes out on top of every situation. He is the Polar opposite of his fearful colleague. Just like a Spartan warrior, a passionate businessman does not cringe in the face of (Commercial) battles. His indefatigable resolve to succeed is total.

Passion pushes you to rise earlier than others and set about the day's activities; it brings out the creative genius in you; pumps adrenaline through your system whenever thoughts of your enterprise flash through your mind; and sets you on the path to productive action and the actualization of your goals. No business can truly succeed without the passionate disposition of its owner to its operation.

REVERSAL: *Passion for a particular activity or product should not be the main reason for starting a business. You must examine the market, potential demand, competition, resources required to enter the market, and the uniqueness of the idea.*

ABOUT THE AUTHOR

Comrade Jude. O Obuseh is the founder and Executive Director of Conflict Prevention and Peace Building Initiative, CPPBI, a Non-Governmental Organization committed to the prevention of violent conflicts in Nigeria and Africa, and JOVAB Group, a business mentorship and investment platform committed to creating Africa's next set of digital entrepreneurs.